Discover
Explore
Experience
Pray

Go Deep

GO DEEP DISCUSSION NOTEBOOK
BY DIANA BERNS
ROAD MAP MINISTRIES

derek
PUBLISHING

DEREK PUBLISHING

Diana Berns; Go DEEP Discussion Notebook, Copyright © 2022
All rights reserved. Printed in the United States of America.

Requests for information should be addressed to:
Derek Publishing, 2945 Bell Road #145, Auburn, California 95603
derekpublishing.com

Library of Congress Cataloging-in-Publication Data
Names: Diana Berns
Title: Go DEEP Discussion Notebook
Identifiers: ISBN's Workbook: 978-1-946561-39-8
Subjects: Religious / Education / Discipleship

MINISTRIES, INC.

derek
PUBLISHING

J616ROADMAP.ORG   derekpublishing.com

Contents

Discover
Explore
Experience
Pray

About this Notebook

Relationships are vital to our health and growth—spiritually, emotionally and mentally. We are to be transformed by the "renewing of our minds." We were not made to be alone or figure things out on our own.

The Spirit of God will use the Word of God to speak through the people of God, strengthening our faith as we grow in our understanding. Whether you are studying a passage of Scripture or reviewing a Bible based message, God's desire is for us to allow His Word to transform us.

The Go Deep Discussion Notebook will guide you through following the "Principles of Good Bible Study"— observation, interpretation, reflection and application. This pattern develops a framework to engage your community in God focused discussion.

As you commit to "Go Deep" —Discover, Explore, Experience, and Pray — with those in your discussion group, our prayer is that your conversations would be rooted and established in God's Word.

This format is simple and becomes easier with practice. Learning the questions to ask to keep the conversation meaningful comes with time. We hope this tool would be a great benefit to you.

———

Steps to Follow

The format is simple. It can be applied to a Bible based message and used for one-on-one discussion or for a group. It is designed to record both your response and responses from others. When you meet in with your group, begin with prayer and move through the process that follows.

1. BEGIN WITH PRAYER

2. REVIEW THE MESSAGE

Have this notebook with you while you listen to the message. If you have been provided with message notes, you can keep them in your notebook. Record your responses to the following questions.

What was the message about?
What stood out to you?
What were the main points or ideas you remember?

3. Discover

This step utilizes the "Principles of Good Bible Study" observation and interpretation. **Keep your discussion based on the facts.** Bring the conversation back to what was said and what it means by definition. This is not the time for opinions. Go back to the Word or message given as you "Focus on God" and "Focus on Us."

OBSERVE — What does it say? Or what was said?
INTERPRET — What does it mean?

▶ FOCUS ON GOD —

What was said about God, Jesus or Holy Spirit?

NATURE—How was God described? Define the words.
PURPOSES—What has God done, is He doing, or will He do?
PRIORITIES—What does God value?

▶ FOCUS ON US —

What was said about people?

WARNINGS—What do we need to be aware of?
INSTRUCTIONS—What do we need to do?
PROMISES—What can we count on?

4. Explore

This step utilizes the "Principles of Good Bible Study" reflection. You can give a moment during your group time for people to think and write. You do not have to share what you record. It is personal. Without reflection it is difficult to apply the principles discussed to your life. This is where transformation begins.

> REFLECT — What does this mean to me?

▶ FOCUS ON YOU —

Did you identify with the people in the message?
How might you respond in similar situations?

5. Experience

This step utilizes the "Principles of Good Bible Study" application. Applying the Word of God to your life is where you will experience transformation.

> APPLY — What will I do with what I've learned?

Sharing what you've learned and the decisions you've made is an important part of growing together. What will you share? Why is this important to you?

6. Pray

It is a privilege to speak with God on behalf of another. Take time to record what each person in your group is grateful for and any needs they may have. Remember to review next time you meet.

———

Principles of Good Bible Study

OBSERVE > INTERPRET > REFLECT > APPLY

Careful observation leads to accurate interpretation which brings about meaningful reflection causing appropriate application.

———

About Road Map Ministries

The Bible leads us to the Person of Jesus like a road map guides you to a destination. Road Map Ministries, Inc. develops people, products and programs that give clear direction to know God through His Word. Our desire is that those impacted can in turn guide others to follow this path.

Diana Berns, the founder, simply put is a communicator. Her passion is teaching, training and developing programs and products to bring understanding about who God is, what He is doing and what is important to Him. She believes that understanding fosters trust in our relationship with Him and strengthens our ability to boldly walk in faith. She brings spiritual concepts into our physical understanding to awaken a desire to pursue the depths of God.

Her foundation of understanding has been built through relationships and experiences that have taken her to places she never dreamed—Kenya, Tanzania, Ethiopia and Sierra Leone in Africa, and Kerala, Tamil Nadu, Uttar Pradesh in India. She served with Ancient Promise Ministries from its inception in 2008, developing the ministry its programs and curriculum as she grew in her relationship with Jesus.

Diana has three adult children who are all married and producing grandchildren. She current lives in Auburn, California and serves as women's ministry director at Auburn Grace Community Church.

To learn more visit J616roadmap.org

Community

NAME

CONTACT INFO

DATE / TIME

LOCATION

Go Deep

Discover
Explore
Experience
Pray

BEGIN WITH PRAYER

REVIEW THE MESSAGE

What was the message about?
What stood out to you?
What were the main points or ideas you remember?

Discover

OBSERVE
What does it say?
Or what was said?

INTERPRET
What does it mean?

▶ FOCUS ON GOD —

What was said about God, Jesus or Holy Spirit?

How was God described? Define the words.
What has God done, is He doing, or will He do?
What does God value?

_____

_____

_____

_____

_____

_____

_____

_____

_____

_____

_____

_____

_____

_____

_____

_____

▶ FOCUS ON US —

What was said about people?

What do we need to be aware of?
What do we need to do?
What can we count on?

_____

_____

_____

_____

Explore

REFLECT
What does this
mean to me?

▶ FOCUS ON YOU —

Did you identify with the people in the message?
How might you respond in similar situations?

Experience

APPLY
What will I do with
what I've learned?

Sharing what you've learned and the decisions
you've made is an important part of growing together.
What will you share? Why is this important to you?

_____

_____

_____

_____

_____

_____

_____

_____

_____

_____

_____

_____

Pray

It is a privilege to speak with God on behalf of another. Take time to record
what each person in your group is grateful for and any needs they may have.
Remember to review next time you meet.

_____

_____

_____

_____

_____

_____

_____

_____

_____

_____

Go Deep

Discover
Explore
Experience
Pray

REVIEW THE MESSAGE

What was the message about?
What stood out to you?
What were the main points or ideas you remember?

Discover

OBSERVE
What does it say?
Or what was said?

INTERPRET
What does it mean?

▶ FOCUS ON GOD —

What was said about God, Jesus or Holy Spirit?

How was God described? Define the words.
What has God done, is He doing, or will He do?
What does God value?

_____
_____
_____
_____
_____
_____
_____
_____
_____
_____
_____
_____
_____
_____
_____

▶ FOCUS ON US —

What was said about people?

What do we need to be aware of?
What do we need to do?
What can we count on?

_____
_____
_____
_____

Explore

REFLECT
What does this
mean to me?

▶ FOCUS ON YOU —

Did you identify with the people in the message?
How might you respond in similar situations?

Experience

APPLY

What will I do with
what I've learned?

Sharing what you've learned and the decisions
you've made is an important part of growing together.
What will you share? Why is this important to you?

Pray

It is a privilege to speak with God on behalf of another. Take time to record
what each person in your group is grateful for and any needs they may have.
Remember to review next time you meet.

Go Deep

Discover
Explore
Experience
Pray

REVIEW THE MESSAGE

What was the message about?
What stood out to you?
What were the main points or ideas you remember?

Discover

▶ FOCUS ON GOD —

What was said about God, Jesus or Holy Spirit?

> How was God described? Define the words.
> What has God done, is He doing, or will He do?
> What does God value?

OBSERVE
What does it say?
Or what was said?

INTERPRET
What does it mean?

_____

_____

_____

_____

_____

_____

_____

_____

_____

_____

_____

_____

_____

_____

_____

_____

▶ FOCUS ON US —

What was said about people?

> What do we need to be aware of?
> What do we need to do?
> What can we count on?

_____

_____

_____

_____

Explore

> FOCUS ON YOU —

Did you identify with the people in the message?
How might you respond in similar situations?

REFLECT
What does this
mean to me?

Experience

APPLY
What will I do with
what I've learned?

Sharing what you've learned and the decisions
you've made is an important part of growing together.
What will you share? Why is this important to you?

_____

_____

_____

_____

_____

_____

_____

_____

_____

_____

_____

Pray

It is a privilege to speak with God on behalf of another. Take time to record
what each person in your group is grateful for and any needs they may have.
Remember to review next time you meet.

_____

_____

_____

_____

_____

_____

_____

_____

_____

Go Deep

Discover
Explore
Experience
Pray

REVIEW THE MESSAGE

What was the message about?
What stood out to you?
What were the main points or ideas you remember?

Discover

OBSERVE
What does it say?
Or what was said?

INTERPRET
What does it mean?

▶ FOCUS ON GOD —

What was said about God, Jesus or Holy Spirit?

How was God described? Define the words.
What has God done, is He doing, or will He do?
What does God value?

_____

_____

_____

_____

_____

_____

_____

_____

_____

_____

_____

_____

_____

_____

_____

_____

_____

_____

_____

▶ FOCUS ON US —

What was said about people?

What do we need to be aware of?
What do we need to do?
What can we count on?

_____

_____

_____

_____

Explore

REFLECT
What does this
mean to me?

▶ FOCUS ON YOU —

Did you identify with the people in the message?
How might you respond in similar situations?

Experience

APPLY
What will I do with
what I've learned?

Sharing what you've learned and the decisions
you've made is an important part of growing together.
What will you share? Why is this important to you?

_____

_____

_____

_____

_____

_____

_____

_____

_____

_____

_____

Pray

It is a privilege to speak with God on behalf of another. Take time to record
what each person in your group is grateful for and any needs they may have.
Remember to review next time you meet.

_____

_____

_____

_____

_____

_____

_____

_____

_____

Go Deep

Discover
Explore
Experience
Pray

BEGIN WITH PRAYER

REVIEW THE MESSAGE

What was the message about?
What stood out to you?
What were the main points or ideas you remember?

Discover

OBSERVE
What does it say?
Or what was said?
INTERPRET
What does it mean?

▶ FOCUS ON GOD —

What was said about God, Jesus or Holy Spirit?

> How was God described? Define the words.
> What has God done, is He doing, or will He do?
> What does God value?

_____

_____

_____

_____

_____

_____

_____

_____

_____

_____

_____

_____

_____

_____

_____

_____

▶ FOCUS ON US —

What was said about people?

> What do we need to be aware of?
> What do we need to do?
> What can we count on?

_____

_____

_____

_____

Explore

REFLECT
What does this
mean to me?

▶ FOCUS ON YOU —

Did you identify with the people in the message?
How might you respond in similar sit_ations?

Experience

APPLY
What will I do with
what I've learned?

Sharing what you've learned and the decisions
you've made is an important part of growing together.
What will you share? Why is this important to you?

_____

_____

_____

_____

_____

_____

_____

_____

_____

_____

Pray

It is a privilege to speak with God on behalf of another. Take time to record
what each person in your group is grateful for and any needs they may have.
Remember to review next time you meet.

_____

_____

_____

_____

_____

_____

_____

_____

Go Deep

Discover
Explore
Experience
Pray

REVIEW THE MESSAGE

What was the message about?
What stood out to you?
What were the main points or ideas you remember?

Discover

OBSERVE
What does it say?
Or what was said?

INTERPRET
What does it mean?

▶ FOCUS ON GOD —

What was said about God, Jesus or Holy Spirit?

How was God described? Define the words.
What has God done, is He doing, or will He do?
What does God value?

_____

_____

_____

_____

_____

_____

_____

_____

_____

_____

_____

_____

_____

_____

_____

_____

▶ FOCUS ON US —

What was said about people?

What do we need to be aware of?
What do we need to do?
What can we count on?

_____

_____

_____

_____

Explore

REFLECT
What does this
mean to me?

▶ FOCUS ON YOU —

Did you identify with the people in the message?
How might you respond in similar situations?

Experience

APPLY
What will I do with
what I've learned?

Sharing what you've learned and the decisions
you've made is an important part of growing together.
What will you share? Why is this important to you?

_____

_____

_____

_____

_____

_____

_____

_____

_____

_____

Pray

It is a privilege to speak with God on behalf of another. Take time to record
what each person in your group is grateful for and any needs they may have.
Remember to review next time you meet.

_____

_____

_____

_____

_____

_____

_____

_____

Go Deep

Discover
Explore
Experience
Pray

REVIEW THE MESSAGE

What was the message about?
What stood out to you?
What were the main points or ideas you remember?

Discover

OBSERVE
What does it say?
Or what was said?

INTERPRET
What does it mean?

▶ FOCUS ON GOD —

What was said about God, Jesus or Holy Spirit?

How was God described? Define the words.
What has God done, is He doing, or will He do?
What does God value?

_____

_____

_____

_____

_____

_____

_____

_____

_____

_____

_____

_____

_____

_____

▶ FOCUS ON US —

What was said about people?

What do we need to be aware of?
What do we need to do?
What can we count on?

_____

_____

_____

_____

Explore

> FOCUS ON YOU —

Did you identify with the people in the message?
How might you respond in similar situations?

REFLECT
What does this
mean to me?

Experience

APPLY
What will I do with
what I've learned?

Sharing what you've learned and the decisions
you've made is an important part of growing together.
What will you share? Why is this important to you?

Pray

It is a privilege to speak with God on behalf of another. Take time to record
what each person in your group is grateful for and any needs they may have.
Remember to review next time you meet.

Go Deep

Discover
Explore
Experience
Pray

REVIEW THE MESSAGE

What was the message about?
What stood out to you?
What were the main points or ideas you remember?

Discover

OBSERVE
What does it say?
Or what was said?

INTERPRET
What does it mean?

▶ FOCUS ON GOD —

What was said about God, Jesus or Holy Spirit?

How was God described? Define the words.
What has God done, is He doing, or will He do?
What does God value?

_____

_____

_____

_____

_____

_____

_____

_____

_____

_____

_____

_____

_____

_____

_____

_____

▶ FOCUS ON US —

What was said about people?

What do we need to be aware of?
What do we need to do?
What can we count on?

_____

_____

_____

_____

Explore

REFLECT
What does this
mean to me?

▶ FOCUS ON YOU —

Did you identify with the people in the message?
How might you respond in similar situations?

Experience

APPLY
What will I do with
what I've learned?

Sharing what you've learned and the decisions
you've made is an important part of growing together.
What will you share? Why is this important to you?

Pray

It is a privilege to speak with God on behalf of another. Take time to record
what each person in your group is grateful for and any needs they may have.
Remember to review next time you meet.

Go Deep

Discover
Explore
Experience
Pray

BEGIN WITH PRAYER

REVIEW THE MESSAGE

What was the message about?
What stood out to you?
What were the main points or ideas you remember?

Discover

OBSERVE
What does it say?
Or what was said?

INTERPRET
What does it mean?

▶ FOCUS ON GOD —

What was said about God, Jesus or Holy Spirit?

How was God described? Define the words.
What has God done, is He doing, or will He do?
What does God value?

_____

_____

_____

_____

_____

_____

_____

_____

_____

_____

_____

_____

_____

_____

_____

_____

▶ FOCUS ON US —

What was said about people?

What do we need to be aware of?
What do we need to do?
What can we count on?

_____

_____

_____

_____

Explore

REFLECT
What does this
mean to me?

▶ FOCUS ON YOU —

Did you identify with the people in the message?
How might you respond in similar situations?

Experience

APPLY
What will I do with
what I've learned?

Sharing what you've learned and the decisions
you've made is an important part of growing together.
What will you share? Why is this important to you?

_____
_____
_____
_____
_____
_____
_____
_____
_____
_____
_____
_____

Pray

It is a privilege to speak with God on behalf of another. Take time to record
what each person in your group is grateful for and any needs they may have.
Remember to review next time you meet.

_____
_____
_____
_____
_____
_____
_____
_____
_____
_____

Go Deep

Discover
Explore
Experience
Pray

BEGIN WITH PRAYER

REVIEW THE MESSAGE

What was the message about?
What stood out to you?
What were the main points or ideas you remember?

Discover

▶ FOCUS ON GOD —

What was said about God, Jesus or Holy Spirit?

How was God described? Define the words.
What has God done, is He doing, or will He do?
What does God value?

OBSERVE
What does it say?
Or what was said?

INTERPRET
What does it mean?

_____

_____

_____

_____

_____

_____

_____

_____

_____

_____

_____

_____

_____

_____

_____

▶ FOCUS ON US —

What was said about people?

What do we need to be aware of?
What do we need to do?
What can we count on?

_____

_____

_____

_____

Explore

REFLECT
What does this
mean to me?

FOCUS ON YOU —

Did you identify with the people in the message?
How might you respond in similar situations?

Experience

> **APPLY**
> What will I do with
> what I've learned?

Sharing what you've learned and the decisions
you've made is an important part of growing together.
What will you share? Why is this important to you?

_____

_____

_____

_____

_____

_____

_____

_____

_____

_____

_____

Pray

It is a privilege to speak with God on behalf of another. Take time to record
what each person in your group is grateful for and any needs they may have.
Remember to review next time you meet.

_____

_____

_____

_____

_____

_____

_____

_____

Go Deep

Discover
Explore
Experience
Pray

BEGIN WITH PRAYER

REVIEW THE MESSAGE

What was the message about?
What stood out to you?
What were the main points or ideas you remember?

Discover

OBSERVE
What does it say?
Or what was said?

INTERPRET
What does it mean?

▶ FOCUS ON GOD —

What was said about God, Jesus or Holy Spirit?

How was God described? Define the words.
What has God done, is He doing, or will He do?
What does God value?

_____

_____

_____

_____

_____

_____

_____

_____

_____

_____

_____

_____

_____

_____

_____

▶ FOCUS ON US —

What was said about people?

What do we need to be aware of?
What do we need to do?
What can we count on?

_____

_____

_____

Explore

REFLECT
What does this
mean to me?

▶ FOCUS ON YOU —

Did you identify with the people in the message?
How might you respond in similar situations?

Experience

APPLY
What will I do with
what I've learned?

Sharing what you've learned and the decisions
you've made is an important part of growing together.
What will you share? Why is this important to you?

_____

_____

_____

_____

_____

_____

_____

_____

_____

_____

_____

Pray

It is a privilege to speak with God on behalf of another. Take time to record
what each person in your group is grateful for and any needs they may have.
Remember to review next time you meet.

_____

_____

_____

_____

_____

_____

_____

_____

Go Deep

Discover
Explore
Experience
Pray

REVIEW THE MESSAGE

What was the message about?
What stood out to you?
What were the main points or ideas you remember?

Discover

OBSERVE
What does it say?
Or what was said?

INTERPRET
What does it mean?

▶ FOCUS ON GOD —

What was said about God, Jesus or Holy Spirit?

> How was God described? Define the words.
> What has God done, is He doing, or will He do?
> What does God value?

_____

_____

_____

_____

_____

_____

_____

_____

_____

_____

_____

_____

_____

_____

_____

▶ FOCUS ON US —

What was said about people?

> What do we need to be aware of?
> What do we need to do?
> What can we count on?

_____

_____

_____

_____

Explore

> FOCUS ON YOU —

Did you identify with the people in the message?
How might you respond in similar situations?

REFLECT
What does this
mean to me?

Experience

APPLY
What will I do with
what I've learned?

Sharing what you've learned and the decisions
you've made is an important part of growing together.
What will you share? Why is this important to you?

_____

_____

_____

_____

_____

_____

_____

_____

_____

_____

_____

_____

Pray

It is a privilege to speak with God on behalf of another. Take time to record
what each person in your group is grateful for and any needs they may have.
Remember to review next time you meet.

_____

_____

_____

_____

_____

_____

_____

_____

_____

Go Deep

Discover
Explore
Experience
Pray

BEGIN WITH PRAYER

REVIEW THE MESSAGE

What was the message about?
What stood out to you?
What were the main points or ideas you remember?

Discover

OBSERVE
What does it say?
Or what was said?

INTERPRET
What does it mean?

▶ FOCUS ON GOD —

What was said about God, Jesus or Holy Spirit?

How was God described? Define the words.
What has God done, is He doing, or will He do?
What does God value?

_____

_____

_____

_____

_____

_____

_____

_____

_____

_____

_____

_____

_____

_____

▶ FOCUS ON US —

What was said about people?

What do we need to be aware of?
What do we need to do?
What can we count on?

_____

_____

_____

_____

Explore

REFLECT
What does this
mean to me?

▶ FOCUS ON YOU —

Did you identify with the people in the message?
How might you respond in similar situations?

Experience

APPLY
What will I do with
what I've learned?

Sharing what you've learned and the decisions
you've made is an important part of growing together.
What will you share? Why is this important to you?

_____

_____

_____

_____

_____

_____

_____

_____

_____

_____

_____

Pray

It is a privilege to speak with God on behalf of another. Take time to record
what each person in your group is grateful for and any needs they may have.
Remember to review next time you meet.

_____

_____

_____

_____

_____

_____

_____

_____

_____

_____

Go Deep

Discover
Explore
Experience
Pray

REVIEW THE MESSAGE

What was the message about?
What stood out to you?
What were the main points or ideas you remember?

Discover

OBSERVE
What does it say?
Or what was said?

INTERPRET
What does it mean?

▶ FOCUS ON GOD —

What was said about God, Jesus or Holy Spirit?

How was God described? Define the words.
What has God done, is He doing, or will He do?
What does God value?

_____

_____

_____

_____

_____

_____

_____

_____

_____

_____

_____

_____

_____

_____

_____

_____

▶ FOCUS ON US —

What was said about people?

What do we need to be aware of?
What do we need to do?
What can we count on?

_____

_____

_____

Explore

REFLECT
What does this
mean to me?

▶ FOCUS ON YOU —

Did you identify with the people in the message?
How might you respond in similar situations?

Experience

APPLY
What will I do with
what I've learned?

Sharing what you've learned and the decisions
you've made is an important part of growing together.
What will you share? Why is this important to you?

_____

_____

_____

_____

_____

_____

_____

_____

_____

_____

Pray

It is a privilege to speak with God on behalf of another. Take time to record
what each person in your group is grateful for and any needs they may have.
Remember to review next time you meet.

_____

_____

_____

_____

_____

_____

_____

_____

Go Deep

Discover
Explore
Experience
Pray

REVIEW THE MESSAGE

What was the message about?
What stood out to you?
What were the main points or ideas you remember?

Discover

OBSERVE
What does it say?
Or what was said?

INTERPRET
What does it mean?

▶ FOCUS ON GOD —

What was said about God, Jesus or Holy Spirit?

　　How was God described? Define the words.
　　What has God done, is He doing, or will He do?
　　What does God value?

_____

_____

_____

_____

_____

_____

_____

_____

_____

_____

_____

_____

_____

_____

▶ FOCUS ON US —

What was said about people?

　　What do we need to be aware of?
　　What do we need to do?
　　What can we count on?

_____

_____

_____

_____

Explore

REFLECT
What does this
mean to me?

▶ FOCUS ON YOU —

Did you identify with the people in the message?
How might you respond in similar situations?

Experience

APPLY
What will I do with
what I've learned?

Sharing what you've learned and the decisions
you've made is an important part of growing together.
What will you share? Why is this important to you?

_____

_____

_____

_____

_____

_____

_____

_____

_____

_____

_____

Pray

It is a privilege to speak with God on behalf of another. Take time to record
what each person in your group is grateful for and any needs they may have.
Remember to review next time you meet.

_____

_____

_____

_____

_____

_____

_____

_____

_____

Go Deep

Discover
Explore
Experience
Pray

REVIEW THE MESSAGE

What was the message about?
What stood out to you?
What were the main points or ideas you remember?

Discover

OBSERVE
What does it say?
Or what was said?

INTERPRET
What does it mean?

▶ FOCUS ON GOD —

What was said about God, Jesus or Holy Spirit?

How was God described? Define the words.
What has God done, is He doing, or will He do?
What does God value?

▶ FOCUS ON US —

What was said about people?

What do we need to be aware of?
What do we need to do?
What can we count on?

Explore

REFLECT
What does this
mean to me?

▶ FOCUS ON YOU —

Did you identify with the people in the message?
How might you respond in similar situations?

Experience

APPLY
What will I do with
what I've learned?

Sharing what you've learned and the decisions
you've made is an important part of growing together.
What will you share? Why is this important to you?

_____

_____

_____

_____

_____

_____

_____

_____

_____

_____

Pray

It is a privilege to speak with God on behalf of another. Take time to record
what each person in your group is grateful for and any needs they may have.
Remember to review next time you meet.

_____

_____

_____

_____

_____

_____

_____

_____

_____

Go Deep

Discover
Explore
Experience
Pray

REVIEW THE MESSAGE

What was the message about?
What stood out to you?
What were the main points or ideas you remember?

Discover

OBSERVE
What does it say?
Or what was said?

INTERPRET
What does it mean?

▶ FOCUS ON GOD —

What was said about God, Jesus or Holy Spirit?

How was God described? Define the words.
What has God done, is He doing, or will He do?
What does God value?

_____

_____

_____

_____

_____

_____

_____

_____

_____

_____

_____

_____

_____

_____

▶ FOCUS ON US —

What was said about people?

What do we need to be aware of?
What do we need to do?
What can we count on?

_____

_____

_____

_____

Explore

▶ FOCUS ON YOU —

Did you identify with the people in the message?
How might you respond in similar situations?

Experience

APPLY
What will I do with
what I've learned?

Sharing what you've learned and the decisions
you've made is an important part of growing together.
What will you share? Why is this important to you?

Pray

It is a privilege to speak with God on behalf of another. Take time to record
what each person in your group is grateful for and any needs they may have.
Remember to review next time you meet.

Go Deep

Discover
Explore
Experience
Pray

REVIEW THE MESSAGE

What was the message about?
What stood out to you?
What were the main points or ideas you remember?

Discover

OBSERVE
What does it say?
Or what was said?

INTERPRET
What does it mean?

▶ FOCUS ON GOD —

What was said about God, Jesus or Holy Spirit?

> How was God described? Define the words.
> What has God done, is He doing, or will He do?
> What does God value?

_____

_____

_____

_____

_____

_____

_____

_____

_____

_____

_____

_____

_____

_____

_____

_____

_____

▶ FOCUS ON US —

What was said about people?

> What do we need to be aware of?
> What do we need to do?
> What can we count on?

_____

_____

_____

Explore

> FOCUS ON YOU —

Did you identify with the people in the message?
How might you respond in similar situations?

REFLECT
What does this
mean to me?

Experience

APPLY
What will I do with
what I've learned?

Sharing what you've learned and the decisions
you've made is an important part of growing together.
What will you share? Why is this important to you?

_____

_____

_____

_____

_____

_____

_____

_____

_____

_____

_____

Pray

It is a privilege to speak with God on behalf of another. Take time to record
what each person in your group is grateful for and any needs they may have.
Remember to review next time you meet.

_____

_____

_____

_____

_____

_____

_____

_____

_____

Discover God Together™
Tools and Training

Order Products through Derek Publishing @
derekpublishing.com

Schedule Classes through Road Map Ministries, Inc. @
j616roadmap.org

Made in the USA
Las Vegas, NV
28 August 2023